Deese

Opossums

Opossums

Sandra Lee

THE CHILD'S WORLD®, INC.

Library of Congress Cataloging-in-Publication Data
Lee, Sandra.
Opossums/ by Sandra Lee.
p.   cm.
Includes index.
Summary: Discusses the physical characteristics,
behavior, habitat, and life cycle of opossums.
ISBN 1-56766-480-6 (lib. reinforced : alk. paper)
1. Opossums—Juvenile literature.
[1. Opossums.]   I Title.
QL737.M34L4   1998
599.2'76—dc21   97-35222
CIP
AC

Photo Credits

© David Davis: 10, 30
© 1996 Darrell Gulin/Dembinsky Photo Assoc. Inc.: 6
© 1997 Ed Kanze/Dembinsky Photo Assoc. Inc.: 13
© 1997 Gary Meszaros/Dembinsky Photo Assoc. Inc.: 9
© Gene Boaz: cover
© Joe McDonåld: 15, 20, 23
© Leonard Lee Rue III, The National Audubon Society Collection/PR: 29
© Robert and Linda Mitchell: 24, 26
© Russ Kinne/Comstock, Inc.: 16, 19
© 1992 Skip Moody/Dembinsky Photo Assoc. Inc.: 2

On the cover...

Front cover: This opossum is resting in a tree on a cold winter day.
Page 2: These young opossums are hunting at night.

Table of Contents

Chapter	Page
Meet the Opossum!	7
What Are Opossums?	8
What Do Opossums Look Like?	11
Where Do Opossums Live?	17
How Do Opossums Protect Themselves?	21
What Are Baby Opossums Like?	25
Index & Glossary	32

Have you ever "played possum"? Playing possum means staying very still and pretending to be asleep. Where does the name come from? It comes from a strange animal that plays this trick on its enemies. When an enemy comes near, the animal drops to the ground and plays dead. What is this strange animal? It's an opossum!

What Are Opossums?

Opossums belong to a group of animals called **marsupials**. Marsupials carry their babies in a pouch on their belly. Kangaroos and koalas are marsupials, too. Most marsupials live in Australia or Asia, but the opossum lives in North, Central, and South America.

Opossums are also **mammals**. Mammals are animals that have hair all over their bodies. They have warm blood and feed their babies milk from their bodies. Cats, dogs, and people are mammals, too.

This opossum is sitting on a branch on a cold winter day. ⇒

There are many different kinds of opossums. The best known is called the *Virginia opossum* or *common opossum*. It is the only marsupial that lives in North America. It is about the size of a cat or small dog, but it looks more like a rat. It has four short legs and large, hairless ears that fold up when the animal sleeps.

The common opossum's face is white and pointed, with long whiskers and large, black eyes. The rest of its body is covered with thick, rough fur, usually brown or black.

The opossum's paws have five fingers or toes that all have claws. Its hind feet are almost like human hands. The foot's big toe acts much like our thumb and can grab onto things.

This opossum's paw helps it to grab onto things. ⇒

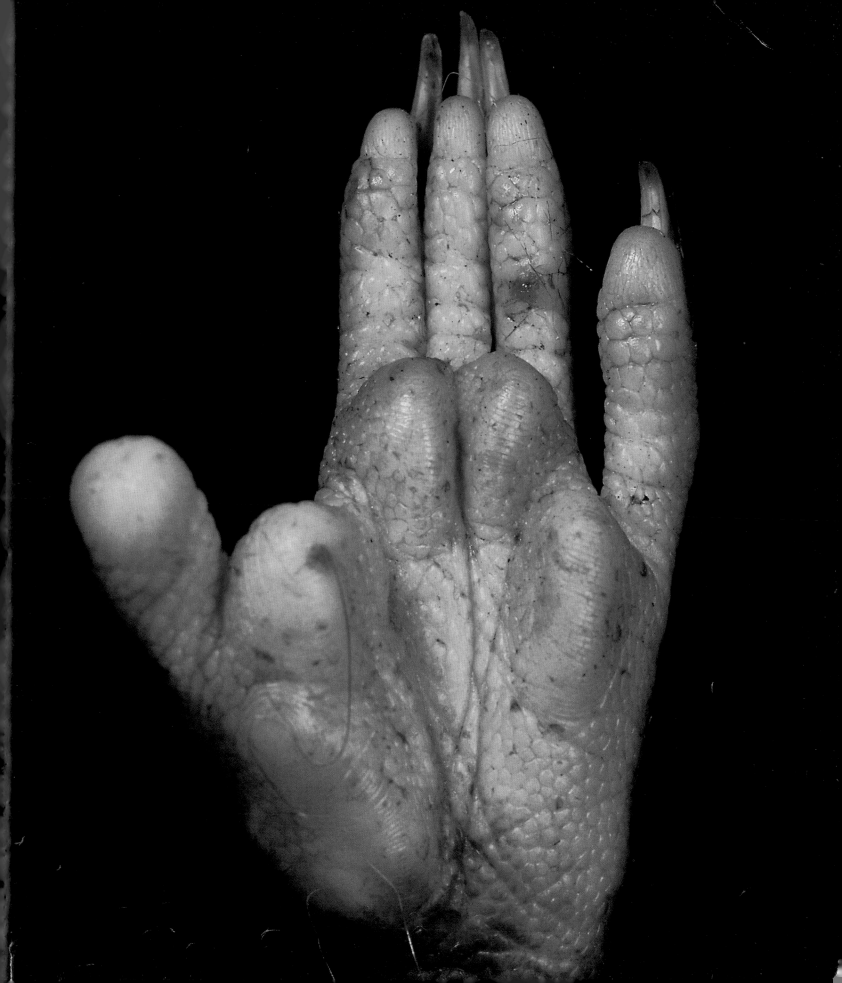

The opossum's hairless tail is long and scaly. It is almost as long as its body. It is called a **prehensile** tail, which means it can wrap tightly around tree branches and other objects. It acts almost like another hand. A young opossum can hang from a tree using only its tail!

This opossum's tail is wrapped around a branch. ⇒

Opossums prefer to live in wooded, bushy areas near rivers. They are not fussy about where they make their homes. They might live in a hollow tree, under a root, or in a hole in the ground. They build their nests out of dead leaves. The opossum picks up the leaves with its mouth and passes them between its front legs. Then it folds its tail under its body and holds the leaves between its belly and its tail.

Opossums are **nocturnal**, which means they are active mostly at night and sleep during the day. They have a very good sense of smell, so they keep their noses to the ground as they go about looking for food. Most anything makes a meal for an opossum—insects, frogs, birds, worms, even garbage!

⇐ This young opossum is sniffing the ground for things to eat.

Opossums have excellent hearing. At the slightest noise they raise their heads to investigate. They have many enemies to watch out for. Owls, bobcats, coyotes, hawks, and other animals eat opossums. And people sometimes hunt opossums for their fur or their meat.

This opossum is climbing a tree to rest for the day. ⇒

How Do Opossums Protect Themselves?

Opossums have a very foul smell, so some animals do not bother to attack them. When an opossum is threatened, however, it tries to scare off its enemy. It growls and shows its 50 sharp teeth. If that doesn't work, it "plays possum," or plays dead. Many of its enemies will not eat an animal that is already dead.

⇐ This frightened opossum is hissing to scare its attacker.

The opossum does a very good job of playing dead! It falls onto its side with its tail rolled up. Its eyes and mouth are wide open and its tongue hangs out. The opossum stays that way until the enemy thinks it is dead. That might mean playing dead for several minutes—or several hours! Eventually the enemy loses interest and leaves. When the opossum thinks it is safe, it "recovers" and moves along!

This opossum is playing dead to escape danger. ⇒

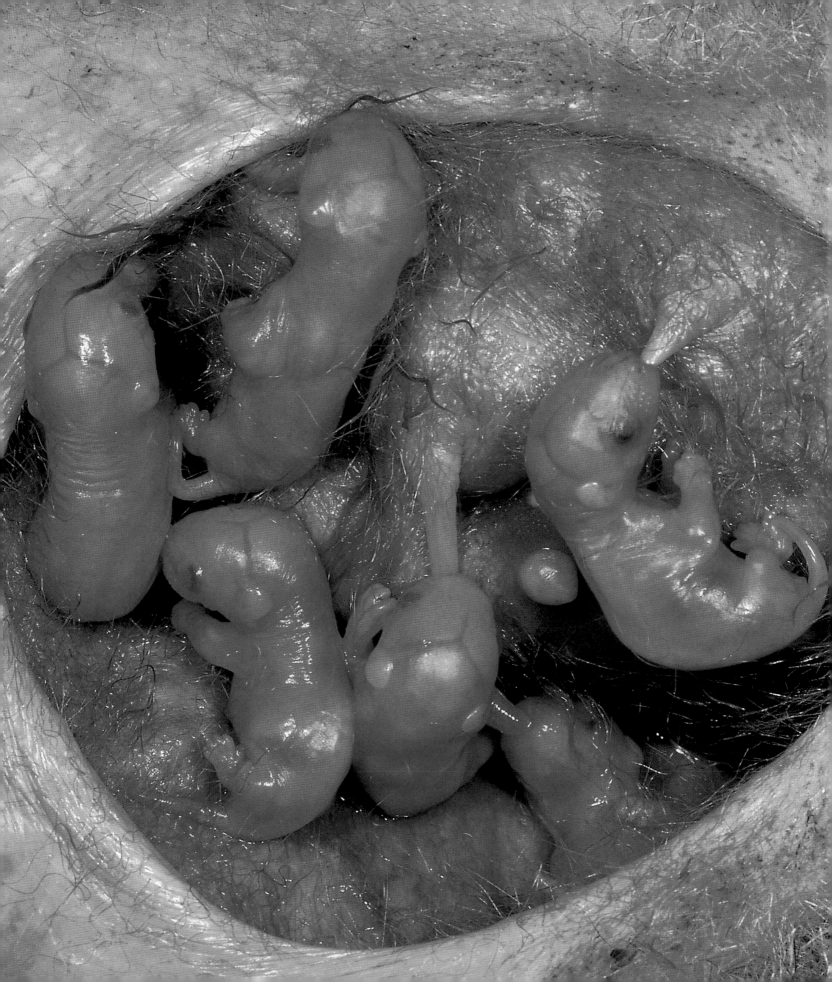

What Are Baby Opossums Like?

Opossums live for only about two years, and they live most of their lives alone. The male and female come together only to mate. When they are born, opossum babies are very tiny and not fully developed. In fact, they are so tiny that 24 of them would fit into a teaspoon!

⇐ These baby opossums are not fully developed.

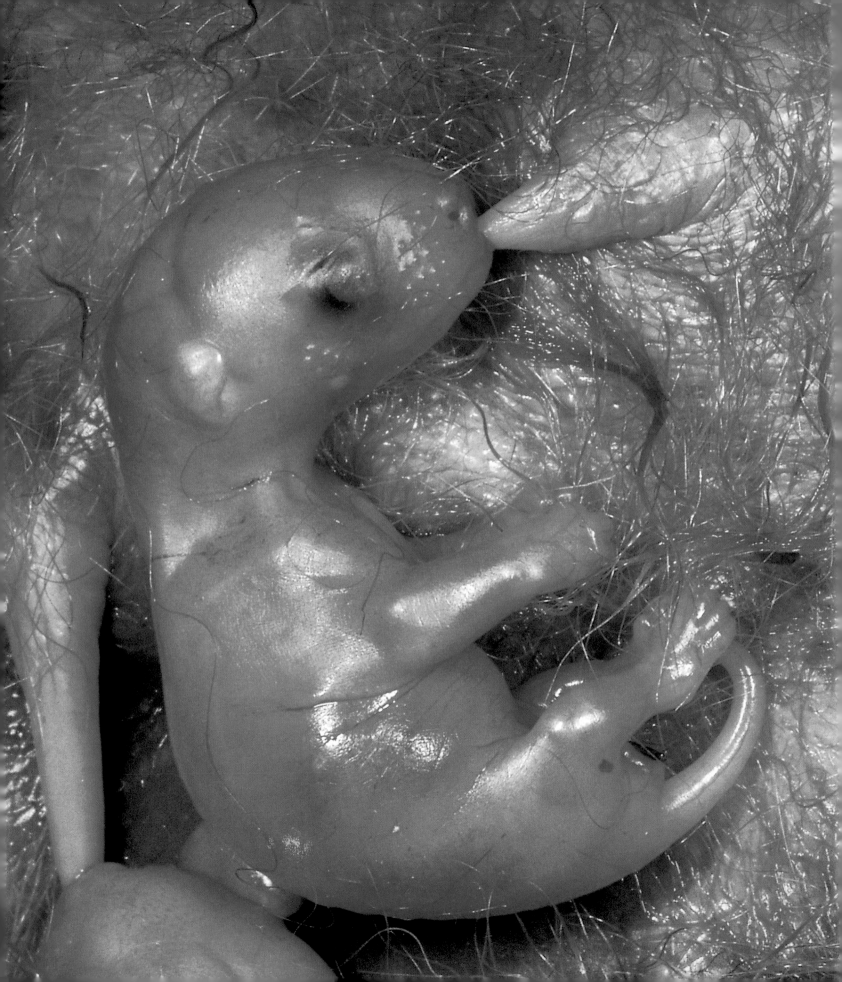

After birth, these tiny babies must make their way to their mother's pouch. There they will grow some more. The trip to the pouch is only about two inches, but that is a very long journey for such a little animal. The baby opossum uses its front legs to pull itself into the pouch.

In the pouch, the mother has 13 **teats** that provide milk for the babies. Each baby attaches itself to a teat. The teat swells like a knob so the baby cannot fall away. The baby stays in the pouch, growing rapidly, for about 60 days.

⇐ This newborn opossum is attached to a teat.

When the babies are big enough, they leave the pouch, but they still stay with their mother. In fact, when the mother goes hunting, she carries her babies on her back. That is a very difficult task if she has a large family! In only about 100 days, the babies are ready to go off on their own.

Baby opossums like these often ride on their mother's backs. ⇒

Since opossums are awake at night, they can be hard to see. But if you are quiet and know where to look, you may spot a few of these wonderful animals. So the next time you are out at night, listen for movements in the bushes. If you are very still, you may see a hungry opossum out for its nighttime walk!

Glossary

mammals (MA–mullz)
Mammals are animals that have hair, warm bodies, and feed their babies milk from their bodies. Cats, dogs, people, and opossums are all mammals.

marsupial (mar-SOO-pee-ull)
A marsupial is an animal that carries its young in a pouch. Opossums, kangaroos, and koalas are all marsupials.

nocturnal (nok-TUR-null)
Nocturnal animals are active at night and sleep during the day. Opossums are nocturnal.

prehensile (pre-HEN-sill)
A prehensile tail can wrap around things and grab onto them. Monkeys and opossums have prehensile tails.

teat (TEET)
A mother's teat produces milk for her babies. Mother opossums have 13 teats inside their pouch.

Index

appearance, 8, 11-12

defenses, 21

enemies, 18

food, 17

location of, 17

mammals, 8

marsupials, 8, 11

nocturnal, 17

paws, 12

playing dead, 7, 21-22

pouch, 8, 27

tail, 14

teat, 27

Virginia opossum, 11

young, 25, 27-28